my first

SCRABBLE®

words

Sing 'Happy Birthday'

by Liz Attenborough

MADCAP

Other titles in this series are

My First SCRABBLE® Words Go Shopping
My First SCRABBLE® Words Say 'Let's Play'
My First SCRABBLE® Words Go to the Seaside

NOTE TO PARENTS

Reading is fun. Reading is also a vital life skill, but is a skill that children will learn more effectively if their learning is pleasurable. You can help them find out about words through playing My First SCRABBLE® Words, through hearing the rhythms of poetry and through experiencing stories that are entertaining. This will speed up the learning process for them and ensure that they know that reading is an activity they really want to do.

First published in Great Britain by Madcap Books, André Deutsch Ltd, 106 Great Russell Street, London WC1B 3LJ
André Deutsch Ltd is a subsidiary of VCI plc

Text and illustrations copyright © 1997 Madcap Books
Cartoon character copyright © 1996 J.W. Spear & Sons plc

Illustrated by Andy Robb
SCRABBLE® is a registered trade mark of J.W. Spear & Sons plc

A catalogue record for this title is available from the British Library
ISBN 0 233 99131 X

Meet the Wordmakers of Alphabet Farm.

Here is Cat.

Here is Dog.

Here is Fox.

Here is Hen.

What words do they need to make when they plan a birthday party?

cake

egg

candle

present

jelly

tea

party

balloon

spoon

It was a lovely sunny morning at Alphabet Farm.

Dog was sweeping.

Cat was sleeping.

Fox was picking cherries.

Hen was picking berries.

And what was Duck doing?

She was swimming round and round her pond, humming a happy tune.

Dog stopped sweeping.
'What is that tune? I'm sure I know it,' he said to Hen.

'Yes, I think I know it too,' she said, 'but I can't remember what it is.'

'Goodness, goodness!' Fox screamed so loudly that he woke Cat. 'I know what that tune is! Come over here.'

'That song is "Happy Birthday"!' Fox said in a loud whisper. 'It must be Duck's birthday TODAY. I thought it was next week. Quick, quick, I must bake a cake and we must have a party!'

'Oh, what fun,' said Dog. 'I love parties.'

'A party! Oh, I love parties, too,' said Hen. 'But there will be so much to do! The party must be a surprise for Duck, so no one must tell her.'

What a fuss and a rush on the Farm, as Hen went round telling all the animals to come to a surprise party at 4 o'clock.

Cat and Dog got ready for the party, too. They blew up balloons and decorated the trees.

'I can't wait for the party to begin,' said Dog.

'I don't mind my sleep being disturbed if it's to help with something as jolly as a birthday party,' said Cat.

Fox raided the kitchen cupboards to make a cake. 'Eggs! Butter! Flour! Chocolate! And more chocolate!'

And Duck kept swimming round and round, humming that special tune.

Soon the kitchen was like a party itself. Fox brought the cake out of the oven, smelling delicious. 'Yummy, yummy!' he said.

'Can I help with the chocolate topping?' said Dog, putting his paws into the bowl.

'Out of the way while I make this jelly,' said Hen. 'Oh, there's so much to do, and so little time.'

'What about a present?' said Cat. 'We will have to make something special. Come on, Dog. Come and help me.'

Cat went outside to get started on the present. She had an idea, and needed to collect some things to make her present for Duck.

'What are we going to make with all that?' asked Dog.

Meanwhile, Duck kept swimming round and round her pond, singing that same song.

Did she know what everyone else was doing?

Suddenly, Fox came running to the pond. 'Come on, everyone,' he shouted. 'Come on! Hurry now, hurry!'

The animals at Alphabet Farm came running to the pond, and they stood at the edge and looked at Duck.

Fox stood on a box. 'Duck,' he started, 'we wish to say Happy Birthday, dear friend, and to give you these presents. And we hope you like parties.'

'Surprise!' shouted Hen, Cat and Dog.

'Come on, everyone, sing, sing!' said Fox.

So the sound of the Happy Birthday song rang loudly round the pond.

'What a lovely surprise!' said Duck. 'I didn't think you had remembered.'

'Open your presents,' said Dog, looking as if he wanted to open them himself.

'Oh, what a gorgeous hat! It's perfect. Thank you,' said Duck as she carefully put the hat on her head.

'Blow out the candles and cut the cake,' said Fox. 'I'm really hungry after all that work.'

'I hope everyone is hungry,' said Duck. 'I didn't know about this wonderful party surprise, so I prepared a birthday tea, too. I was going to surprise you!'

So there were two plates of everything at Duck's birthday party at Alphabet Farm. Can you find two plates with the same food?

'This is fun!' said Duck, eating another piece of cake.

The singing and the eating went on until the sun went down. Some happy animals went to sleep that night feeling very full indeed, as they listened to Duck still humming the Happy Birthday tune.

The Pie

Who made the pie?
I did.
Who stole the pie?
He did.
Who found the pie?
She did.
Who ate the pie?
You did.
Who cried for pie?
We all did.

Anon.